TiGER I

IN ACTION

Norm E Harms

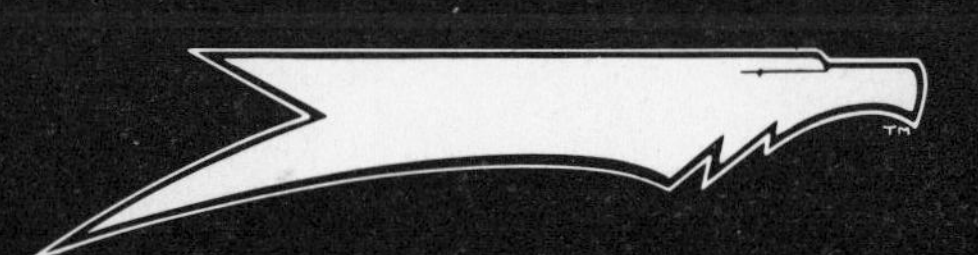

squadron/signal publications

3515 E. TEN MILE ROAD, WARREN, MICHIGAN 48091

The development story of the Panzerkampfwagen VI, Tiger I, has been well documented and detailed in depth in many other previous publications. As such, it is not the intention of this current work to textually recount this area but rather we shall provide for the armor and military enthusiast an overall view using outstanding photographs accompanied by a brief amount of text to show the **TIGERS IN ACTION.**

PHOTO CREDIT:
Bundesarchiv Koblenz
Walter J. Spielberger
Peter Chamberlain Collection
Archiv Kurt Rieger
Archiv Uwe Feist
Norm E. Harms Archiv
Squadron Signal Archiv
Aberdeen Proving Grounds

The period following the fall of France and the shelving of **"Operation Sea Lion,"** the planned German invasion of England, brought a welcomed respite for the panzer divisions. During this time the total number of divisions was doubled, but with nearly a corresponding decrease in the strength of the tank element within the division proper. This reduction in strength had been necessary to establish the new divisions, for overall tank production had lagged, in fact for the whole of 1940 only some 1,000 vehicles had been produced of which only 280 were the first line PzKpfw IV's. Some satisfaction could be derived from the fact that while the tank strength was reduced, technically better pieces were in fact replacing the older models in service. Front line experiences from the Polish and French Campaigns had shown the need for improvement in certain aspects of the tanks themselves, such as additional armor and a more powerful armament. These improvements tended to further slow tank production.

The military situation remained stable until March 1941. The political situation, on the other hand, pressed ever forward. Rumania and Hungary joined the Tripartite Pact with Bulgaria and Yugoslavia following in March 1941. Italy had invaded Greece in October 1940 and her troops were having a most difficult time with the Greeks. Russia pressured for demands which Hitler was not willing to concede, his answer being the preparations for **"Operation Barbarossa,"** the invasion of Russia.

An attempted **coup d' etat** in Yugoslavia after her entry into the Tripartite Pact, and the signing of a friendship pact between Yugoslavia and Russia precipitated immediate German invasion. While German military forces were subduing opposition in Yugoslavia their commitment became further involved by having to assist their Italian ally in Greece and North Africa.

Planning for Barbarossa proceeded, but the invasion could not be initiated until the end of the Greek Campaign, at which time the military forces could be moved back and made ready for the invasion. Those forces in North Africa, under the command of General Rommel, were held to a minimum. They were intended to be a holding force and no great attention placed in this theater of operations. The time delay incurred due to the Yugoslav and Greek involvements meant that operations against Russia could not begin before June, late in the year for beginning such an undertaking. At that time, however, the German High Command felt that only eight to ten weeks would be required to bring Russia to her knees. It seems that the past glories of Poland and France, and more recently those in the Balkans, victories which had come with relative ease, had lead the High Command to make some rather rash judgements concerning the defeat of the USSR.

The left half of the Feifel air system is clearly illustrated in this rear view of an early model **Tiger I.** Mounted on the rear of the hull, right and left, these air cleaners were to filter dust and other foreign matter from the intake air of the Tiger's engine. Requiring continual maintenance for maximum performance, this system was discontinued on vehicles completed after the withdrawal of forces from North Africa.

General Guderian relates that as early as 1933 he had visited a single Russian tank factory which produced 22 **Christie** type tanks per day. Further apprehension is found when a Russian military commission visited Germany early in 1941. Under Hitler's personal orders they were to be shown everything and anything they wished to see in the German tank industry. When shown the **PzKpfw IV** and told that this was Germany's heaviest tank, the commission members declared that they were being deceived and not shown everything as directed by Hitler. This attitude prompted the conclusion among German manufacturers and ordnance personnel that the Russians must in fact already possess some better tank than did the Germans. Readily admitting the Soviet numerical superiority in tanks, the Germans felt that their own technological abilities would overcome this deficiency.

At 0445 hours June 22, 1941, 3,350 German tanks, organized into panzer corps and panzer armies, crossed the Russian frontier opening "Barbarossa". As in France, armored spearheads knifed deeply into Russian territory, and at first appeared to be a carbon copy of their earlier performance in France. Five months later heavy fighting was still raging. Supply difficulties, a general wearing down of equipment, and combat losses plus the onset of an early winter brought the German advance to a halt.

The successes of this five month period are noteworthy when one considers that the Germans did not possess the superior quality in tanks which at first they believed they had. It is true that the **PzKpfw III** and **IV** held advantages over the older Soviet **T-26** and **BT** models which comprised the bulk of the Soviet tank forces, however during the first weeks of the campaign, the Soviets introduced their new medium tank, the **T-34**, into combat. The T-34 was quickly found to be the best medium tank then in service throughout the world and was a factor which the Germans were not prepared to meet. Had the Russians been able to field large numbers of T-34's at the beginning of the invasion, it is doubtful that the German Army would have made the devestating initial gains that it did. Poor Soviet armoured tactics and the committment of their T-34's to battle in a piecemeal fashion allowed the German forces to take full advantage of their superior organization and tactics. Again, as had happened in France, tactics played the important role. Some 17,000 Soviet armored vehicles had been either destroyed or captured for a loss of 2,700 German vehicles.

Impressive as these figures may be, the fact remained that Germany possessed nothing comparable to the Soviet T-34. If they were to complete their conquest they would be forced to adopt, or create, an equal to the T-34.

The rapid succession of German victories in Poland, the Low Lands, France, Yugoslavia and Greece had the effect of instilling overconfidence in their own skills and weapons. One side effect of this had been to underestimate the strength of the Russians and the length of the proposed campaign. Another effect of this complacency seemed to indicate that no further need existed to replace or better present equipment standards. During the late 1930's some design and development work had been undertaken to produce a successor to the Panzer IV. No great urgency had been placed on this development and work had not progressed beyond the prototype stages. Experimentation did proceed, but at a snail's pace. The rude awakening by the advent of the T-34 burst this pipe dream.

In October 1941, General Guderian forwarded a formal report describing in detail "Encounter Experiences" with the T-34. He requested that a military commission along with industrial leaders and designers be sent immediately to study at first hand the T-34 and talk to the men who had engaged these vehicles in combat. This investigation commission arrived in November.

Seen immediately aft of the Tiger's turret and laying atop the engine deck are the rubber connecting links of the **Feifel** system. Tigers fitted with the Feifel system were known as **Tiger (Tp)** or tropical Tigers. Fixed periscopes, mounted and seen, on the driver's and wireless operator's escape hatches provided additional vision when the tank was "buttoned up".

T-34/76D

Even though the production of the **Tiger** was accomplished in the relatively short period of only fifteen months, additional time was lost in their deployment because crews had to be thoroughly trained in their use. Here, at a training school in Germany, new crews await orders prior to practice maneuvers. Dust covers are still fitted to the **"88's"** and machine-guns. Smoke candle projectors can also be seen to protrude from the turret sides and fore and aft on the chassis.

"Suggested" measures which could be taken to regain German technical supremacy covered a wide range: from the capture of a T-34 factory and continuing production, to duplicating the T-34 in Germany. For reasons of material shortages, speed in production, and ego, it was found impractical to duplicate the T-34 exactly. The solution was found in expanding the tank designs which had been under development to meet current and projected needs. Two tank designs emerged from this decision, a medium in the 30 to 40 ton class armed with a **7.5cm L/48** and incorporating the excellent sloping armor of the T-34. The second design was a more powerful version along traditional German lines, angular placement of armor. Specifications for this version had come directly from Hitler himself and made provisions for heavy armor and the mounting of the **8.8cm high velocity gun,** a version of the famed **Flak 18** and **Flak 36** anti-aircraft guns.

Faced with a potentially disastrous situation, the Germans exhibited their inherent technical capabilities to the fullest, a factor which would be called upon with increasing frequency as the war in the east progressed. The available tank development models were quickly modified to include the new proposals and steps were taken to begin their earliest production. As such, deliveries of the latter of the two proposed designs, now designated **PzKpfw VI Tiger,** commenced in August 1942. Production of the former design, known as **PzKpfw V Panther,** followed in November. Two new German "cats" had been born, their growls were heard around the world.

With the introduction of these "cats" in large numbers, and after elimination of the always present production bugs of a new weapon, Germany not only gained the technical superiority over the Russian T-34 which had been sought, but was able to maintain this superiority over all other Allied tanks. Among its contemporaries, the **Tiger I** represented the most powerful vehicle then in service and was still able to hold its own against the majority of Allied armor at the close of the war.

To counter the **Tiger I,** the Russians introduced their **"JS"** series of heavily armed and armored tanks. The pace of this mini, but desperate, arms race quickened and the Germans were to counter the **"JS"** series with their own **Tiger II,** which represented the heaviest tank in service by any nation throughout the Second World War. British and American answers to the Panther and Tiger I were slower in coming for the Western Allies did not engage the Tiger I until the closing days of the North African campaign or Panthers until operations began in Italy. It was not until the closing weeks of the war in Europe that an American counter to the Tigers and Panther appeared in service, that being the **Pershing** armed with a **90mm gun.**

During the first combat encounters with the Tiger, Western Allied gunners were amazed to see their shots literally bounce from its sides. This rather demoralizing demonstration gave rise to the first of the Tiger legends. As is the case with any legend, a story told over and over again tends to warp out of proportion, the seeming invulnerability of the Tiger grew. It was not impossible to disable or destroy a Tiger, the key lay in learning how - combat experience. By the time of the cross channel invasion of Europe, this experience had been gained by British and U.S. forces engaged in Italy and was used to train those forces soon to land in France. Nevertheless the psychological affect of the Tiger remained and is emphasized by the fact that during the early days of the Normandie invasion, U.S. forces reported almost without exception, all German tanks engaged as being Tigers. This situation soon corrected itself as the troops gained confidence. Thereafter, though, when Tigers were met in combat it was with a great amount of caution and respect for a formidable opponent. The **Tiger** had become a legend in its own time.

■ ■ ■

Armament of the **Tiger I** is centered around the **8.8cm KwK 36,** 56 calibers long, a tank adapted version of the famed **"88"** anti-aircraft gun. The high velocity of this weapon, 810m/sec. (2,657 ft./sec.) allowed for an extremely flat trajectory of the shell coupled with high impact striking the target. Use of the "88" in the Tiger came upon direct orders from Hitler. An improved model of the "88", muzzle velocity increased to some 3,700 ft./sec., was used in the Tiger II.

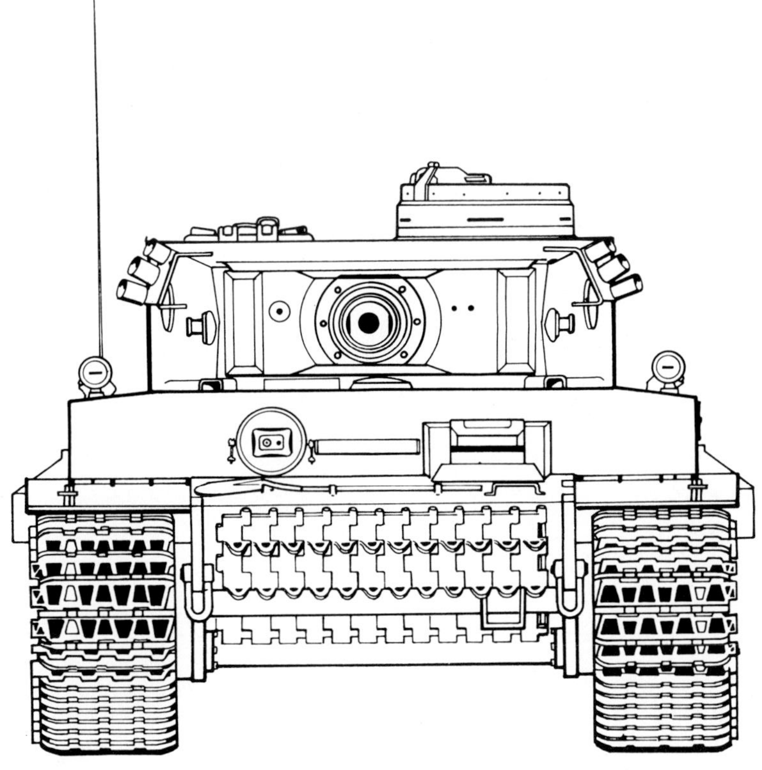

In the foreground, dressed in the distinctive all-black uniform of the Panzertruppe, a **Feldwebel** (U.S. equivalent of Technical Sergeant) records the fall of shot during gunnery practice. The tank commander has already gained considerable combat experience as is indicated by the "Tank Battle Badge" which he wears. Requirements for this award were three engagements with the enemy on different days. Also worn are the "Wound Badge" and "Hitler Youth Proficiency Badge."

The selection of gunnery targets was technically up to the tank commander but the final decision as to fire or not rested with the gunner. This fact may at first sound strange but the Germans realized that while the commander may see a target in a certain respect, the gunner viewed the target from the "gun angle" and was better able to judge the potential effectiveness of the shot.

With final instructions being given by an **Oberfeldwebel** (Master Sergeant), wearing the feldgrau uniform cap, Tiger crews prepare for gunnery practice. Noteworthy are the packages and clips of 7.92mm rifle ammunition viewed in the foreground. The secondary armament of the **Tiger** consisted of two standard **MG 34's**. The interchangeability of rifle and machine-gun ammunition throughout the entire German military greatly assisted in lessening supply difficulties at the front.

The earliest production models of the **Tiger I** did not feature the turret escape hatch, viewed here. In lieu of this hatch, a piston port, similar to that found on the left side of the turret, was to be found. Also absent on the first models was the Feifel air system.

A distinctive advantage which German tank crews held over their Russian counterparts lay in the excellence of communications. This included not only interior tank conversation among the crew themselves but tank to tank communication as well, exemplified by this **Oberleutnant** wearing headset and throat mike. **Panzerbefehls-wagen,** command tank versions, carried various combinations of radios which allowed contact to be maintained with other service branches, such as artillery, and higher level headquarters. Total control played a vital role in German tank tactics.

Driver's visor, located on the left side of the vehicle, could be raised or lowered, as need be, from within the vehicle proper. Immediately to the left of the visor is seen a field modification made to hold additional spare track segments.

(Opposite Page) The **Tiger** hull was divided into four distinctive parts. Forward on the left side, the driver steered the vehicle by means of a steering wheel. Should the need arise, due to an emergency, steering could also be accomplished by using disc brakes activated by two levers on either side of the driver. Seperating the forward two compartments was the transmission gear box, occupying the lower right corner of the photo. The radio operator/machine gunner sat in the right forward compartment being responsible not only for communications but the forward defense of the tank. His ball mounted **MG 34** was hand fired.

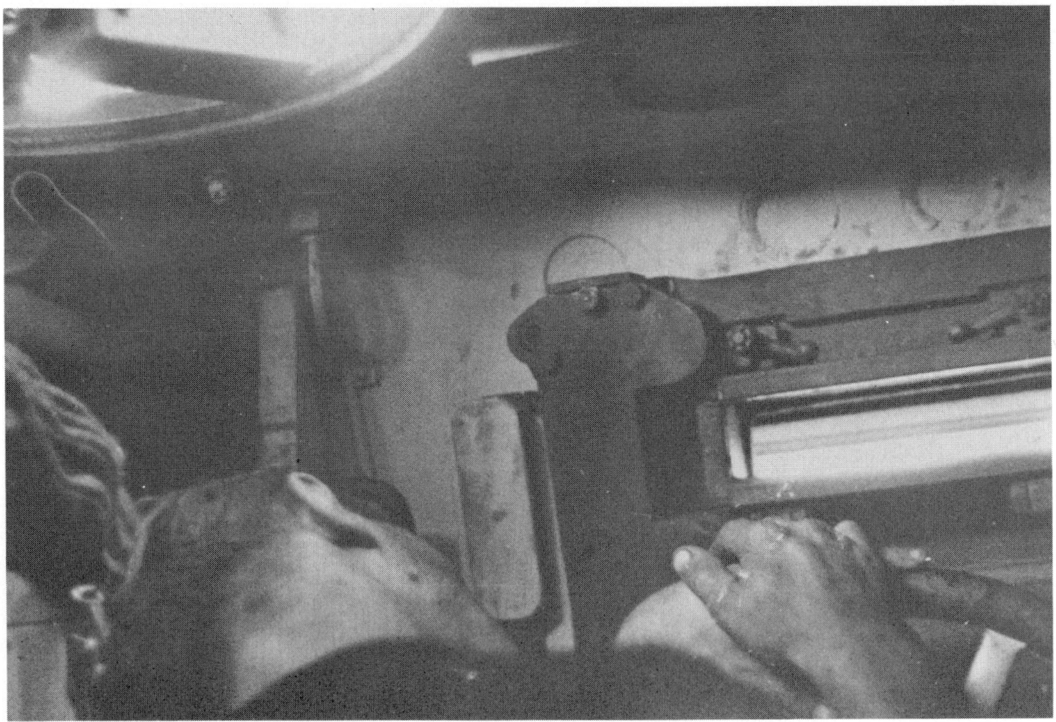

During combat operations, tank crews had to catch up on their sleep as and when they could. Some idea of the confinement found in most tanks is evident from the distance between the driver's head and the overhead portion of the tank hull. These cramped conditions further explain why the driver's and radio operator's escape hatches were located immediately above their respective positions.

The third distinctive part of the **Tiger** hull included the fighting compartment and turret. Here the gunner and loader manned their stations. The second **MG 34** carried by the Tiger was co-axially mounted with the **"88"** and fired by means of a mechanical linkage and foot pedal operated by the gunner. The fifth member of the crew, the commander, was also to be found in the turret position, directly in back and above the gun crew.

The gunner's position in the **Tiger** turret. Elevation and traverse were controlled by handwheels, these operated by the gunner. An additional traverse handwheel, in case of emergency, could also be used by the tank commander. Clearly shown in this illustration are the T.Z.F. 9b sighting telescope, turret position indicator (by clock position) and elevation scale.

General Guderian, second from right, inspects a production model of an early **Tiger I.** His recall to active duty, after having been dismissed by Hitler, and the assumption of the post of Inspector-General of the Armored Troops in February 1943, did much to reform the **Panzertruppen** into the decisive weapon it had once been. A **SS-Hauptsturmführer,** member of the **1. SS-Panzer Division "Leibstandarte SS Adolf Hitler,"** stands to his left.

(Opposite Page) The loader's position in the Tiger turret. From this view we can again see the cramped quarters in which the tank's crew operated. During a battle the loader was undoubtedly the busiest man in the entire crew. Ammunition storage bins for the 92 rounds of **"88"** ammunition are seen immediately under the turret ring. 150 belts of machine-gun ammo were also stored and distributed between the turret and radio operator's position.

Close up of the driver's escape hatch with fixed periscope, gun mantlet and the left side turret trunnion.

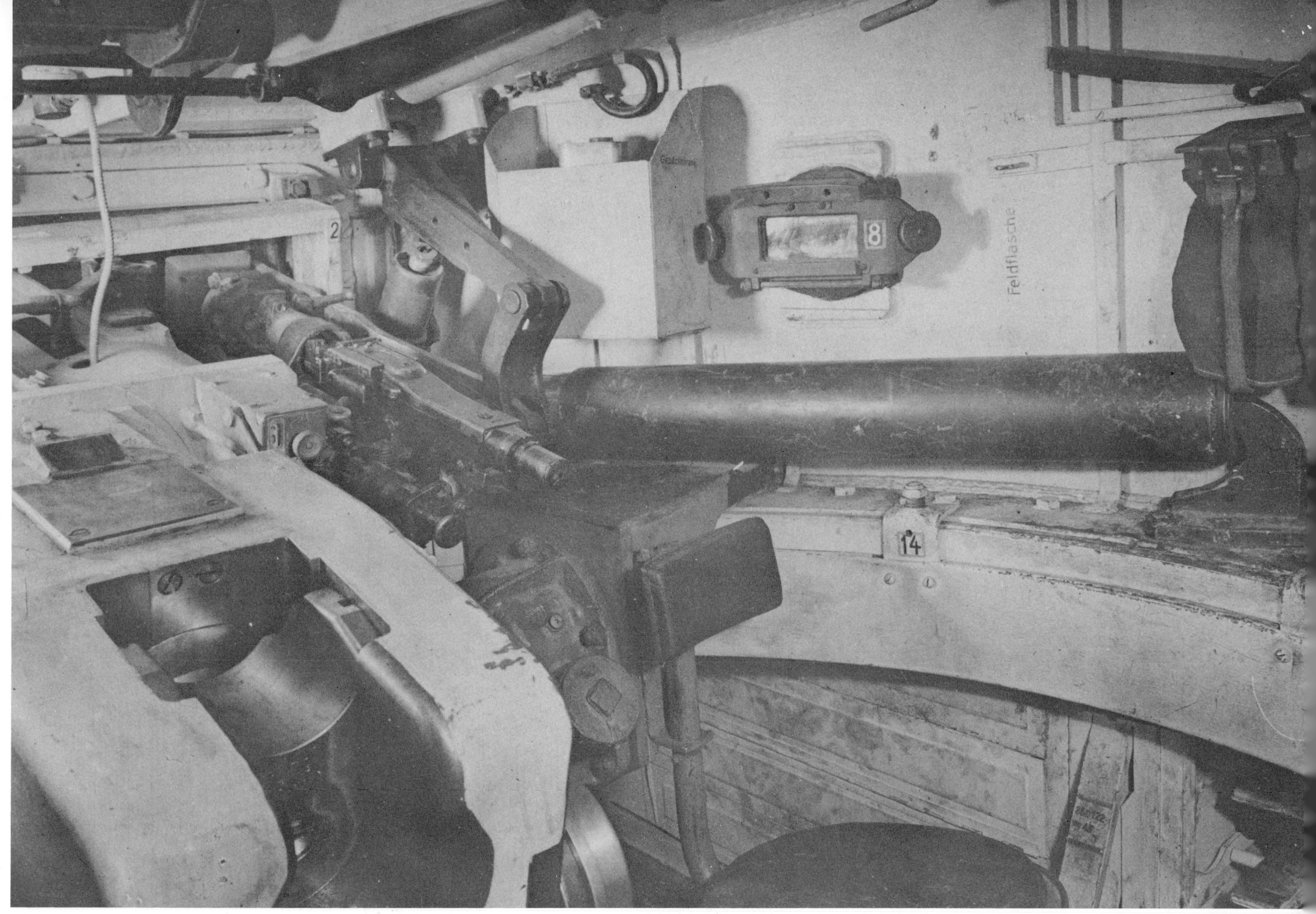
2
8
Feldflasche
14

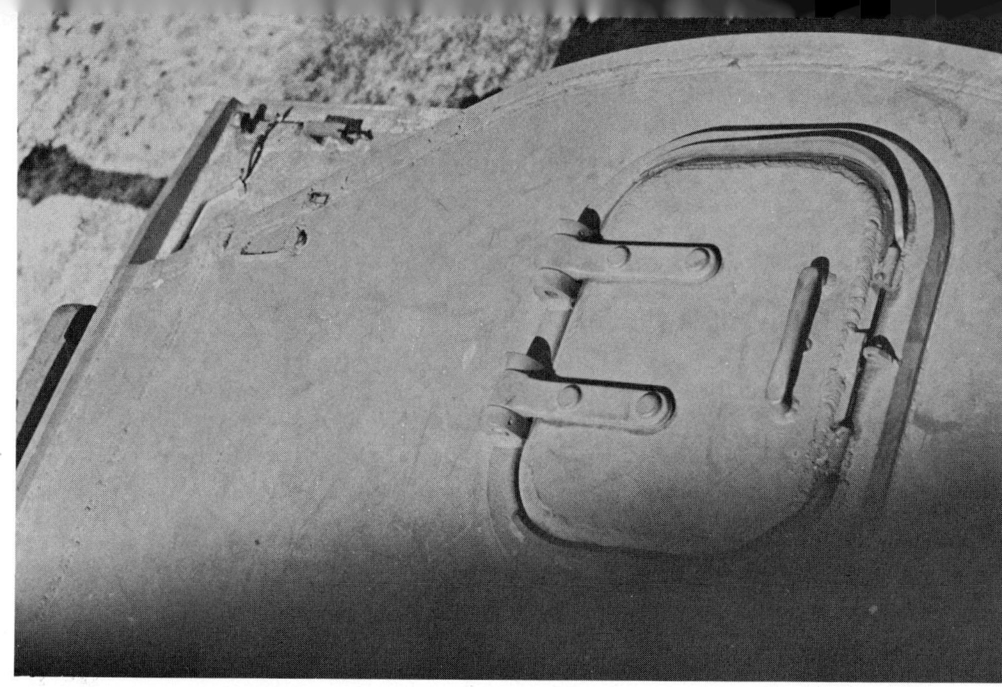

Loader's hatch. While primarily used to pass ammunition into the tank, this hatch could also double for an escape hatch if the rear mounted turret escape hatch were blocked.

(Above Left) This early **Tiger** commander's cupola shows the counter balance spring to assist in opening the hatch and "open position" locking attachment points. The high silhouette and partial blocking of the commander's view was rectified in subsequent models with a cupola similar to that found on the **Panther.**

Both **MG 34's** are seen in this view of the Tiger. Self-defense in close range fighting became increasingly important to the tank crew as the war progressed. This fact had been driven home when the Ferdinand, an offshoot of the Tiger design, suffered heavy losses through enemy troop action when first introduced to combat without self-defense machine gun armament.

Civilian specialists (**Wehrmachtbeamten**) were included within the various German armed forces structures but regarded as separate from them. Uniforms were identical to those of their respective service with changes being made in the service insignia of rank, dark green Waffenfarbe with appropriate secondary color and the letters "V" superimposed on an "H", worn on the shoulder strap. Illustrated here, a **Heereswerkmeister,** assists a Tiger's crew in the field.

Many pieces of equipment have been removed from this **Tiger,** currently on public display at Aberdeen. Enough remains, however, so that we may gain an idea of their placement on the engine deck. The most noticeable feature is the "V" shaped intake ducts into which the rubber connecting links of the Feifel air cleaner were installed. It should be mentioned that the first 495 Tigers produced had been equipped to travel completely submerged up to a depth of 13 feet. The expensive Snorkel equipment, thereafter, being discarded in favor of increased production.

Hanging on the raised engine deck plating, the **Heereswerkmeister** (Army workshop NCO) listens to an engine run-up. "Pop caps", fitted to the exhaust pipes, automatically open when the engine is running, otherwise remain closed to exclude water and other foreign material from entering the exhaust system.

Located on either side of the turret immediately forward of the engine space, are four internal fuel tanks, a total capacity of 141 gallons of gasoline provided the **Tiger** with a cross country range of 42 miles. The fueling cap, marked with an indented "X" can be seen in the upper left hand corner of this photograph.

The large engine deck hatch provided ease of access to the **Tiger's** engine spaces, an important factor when performing field maintenance at the battle front. The size of the hatch can be gauged by comparing the mechanic kneeling on the engine itself.

Inspecting a portion of the Tiger's turret hydraulic systems are (on the left) an **Oberleutnant,** (a Panzer Technical Officer) and a **Wehrmachtbeamter** with the rank of **Heereswerkmeister** (army equivalent rank of senior NCO). The lieutenant's abilities have gone far beyond those normally associated with technical/engineering matters. On his right upper sleeve is seen the "Special Badge For Single-Handed Destruction Of A Tank" in gilt. This award signifies that he has, single-handedly, destroyed five enemy armored fighting vehicles.

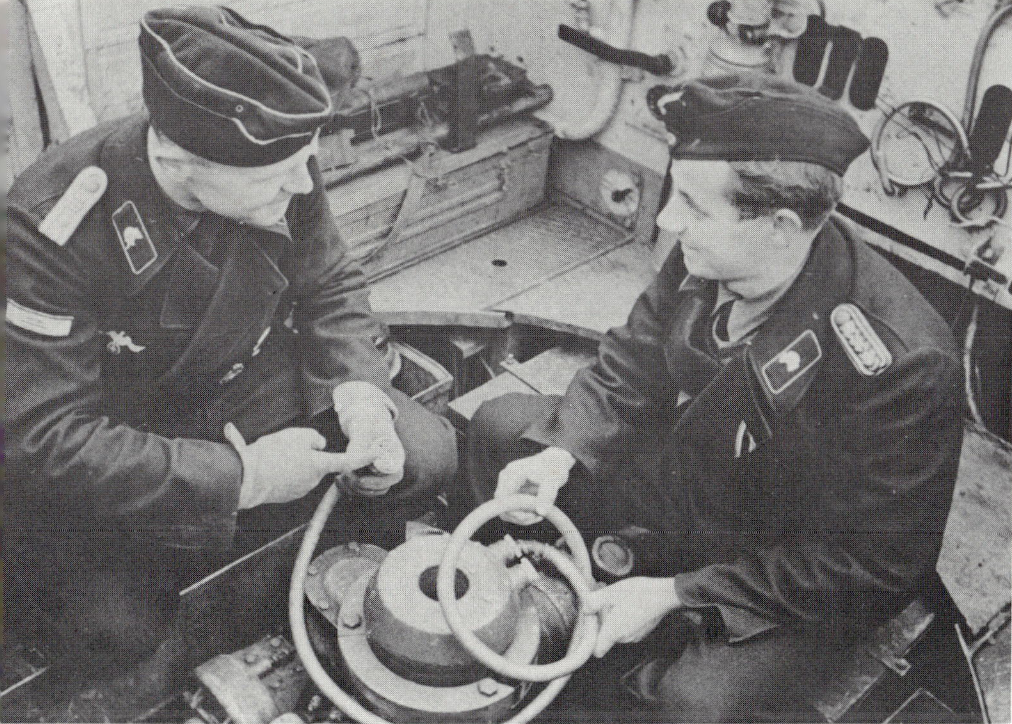

The first 250 production Tigers completed had been fitted with the Maybach V-12 HL 210 P 45 engine. Developing 642 BHP, it soon proved to underpower the **Tiger** and its 62 tons of bulk. The four Solex carburetors are clearly seen in this view.

The remaining 1100 Tigers completed (1376 had been ordered, 1350 delivered by the time production ceased) were powered by the improved Maybach HL 230 P 45 which developed 694 BHP. Even with this improvement, the **Tiger** could only achieve a cross country speed of some 12 MPH.

One of the fundamental German principles concerning maintenance of mechanized equipment directed that such vehicles be repaired as close to the combat front as possible. The validity of this premise is sound. A vehicle which can be repaired "on the spot" is returned to combat more quickly than those which must be sent some distance to the rear for such work.

When local front line maintenance units, divisional level, could not accomplish repairs within a prescribed amount of time, damaged vehicles were withdrawn to rear echelon maintenance depots. Within the German Army, tanks, and self-propelled gun vehicles which could not be repaired within three days were sent to **Stützpunkte** (Field Army Tank Parks). These Parks were more elaborately equipped to facilitate major undertakings, such as the removal of this Tiger's turret.

The Tiger's crew manual stresses the importance of maintaining proper engine oil levels. Lack of oil usually resulted in an overheated engine and fire. With 141 gallons of gasoline and 92 rounds of ammunition on board, the prospects of a fire would tend to be somewhat unnerving.

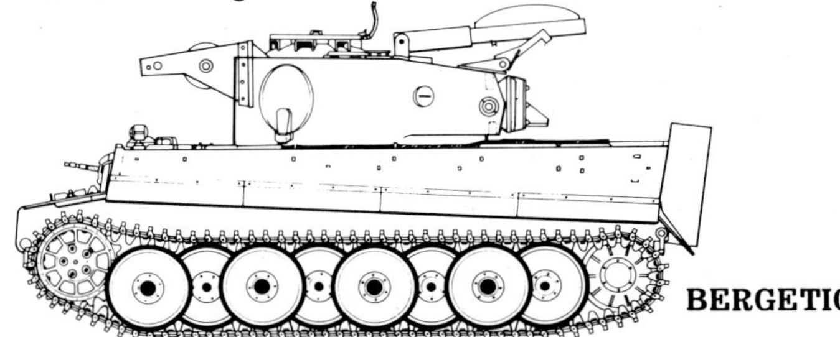

BERGETIGER

Specialized vehicles were required in the recovery of battle damaged tanks. One such vehicle, the 18 ton Schwerer Zugkraftwagen (Sd. Kfz. 9/1), fitted with a 6 ton crane, will be seen to the rear of this Tiger. Prior to the introduction of the heavier tanks, Panther and Tiger, the 18 ton half-track was capable of independent recovery of disabled tanks. Thereafter, recovery vehicles based on Panther, and a few on the Tiger, chassis were used to retrieve their own.

Located on either side of the gun mantlet and on the rear of the turret, the turret trunnions were used to facilitate ease in removing the Tiger's turret. Here the complete turret has been removed from the chassis to undergo major repair. It is interesting to note that the Tiger turret in the background is being given a coat of winter white camouflage before being replaced on its chassis.

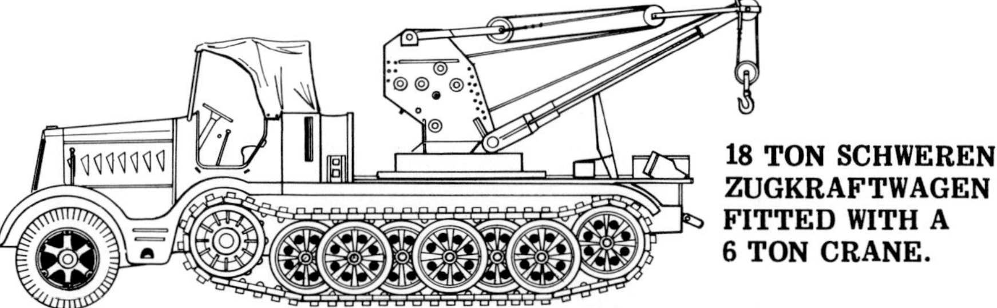

18 TON SCHWEREN ZUGKRAFTWAGEN FITTED WITH A 6 TON CRANE.

Radiators for the water cooled Maybach engine were located on either side of the engine itself. The large grate covered openings on the rear deck allowed air to be drawn through the radiator assisted by two fans per unit. The water filling cap is seen in the upper right hand corner. The mechanic is standing on the engine drive shaft.

Mail call is the highlight of a combat soldier's day. These crew members are wearing reed-green Panzer denim pants. The full Panzer denim suit is two pieced, identical in cut to the black Panzer uniform, and intended for use during summer months.

P.M. (Preventative Maintenance) keeps the tank ready for action at a moments notice. Both the **"88"** and co-axial **MG 34** have been fitted with dust covers, easily removed.

Due to the restricted space within the tank itself, crew members personal belongings were stored in the box located on the rear of the turret. This further explains why the men's steel helmets were secured on the outside of the turret.

The "Panzer Kommandant" (Tank-commander) an Oberleutnant in the type of uniform worn by most Tiger crews.

Obersturmführer Michel Wittman of the "Leibstandarte Adol Hitler", France, June 194

Leutnant of the 501. Schwere Tiger Abteilung in Tunis December, 1942

Tiger "Ladeschütze" (loader) holding the 31 lb. Panzergranate (armor piercing shell). Russia, Summer 1943

Oberscharführer Balthasar Woll, the gunner of Michel Wittmann's TIGER I. Woll is wearing the light weight camouflage uniform of the Waffen SS.

PANZERKAMPFWAGEN VI TIGER I of the s. Panzerabteilung 502, Major Willy Jähde, Woronowo, Russia 1944

PANZERKAMPFWAGEN VI TIGER I Ausf. E of the 1. SS-Panzer-Division "Leibstandarte Adolf Hitler" (LAH). Falaise, August 1944

By the advent of the Second World War, the useful track life of all tanks in general had been greatly extended over those tracks which appeared on the first tanks of WW I. This extension had been accomplished by various means and methods applied to the track design and intergraded with the tank proper. As such, the approximate 20 mile track life of the original British tanks of WW I had been increased to some 500 miles for the heavy tank types of WW II, including the **Tiger.** Medium tanks could expect 1000 to 1300 miles. Here the Tiger's "travel/transport tracks" are being removed for installation of the wider "battle track".

These late model **Tiger I's,** note new cupola and road wheels, stop for the installation of their "battle tracks" before moving to the front. Traffic control and directions are supplied by the two military field policemen (**Feldgendarmerie**), wearing their distinctive gorget, standing on the right. Blackout style headlamp is located between the bow MG and driver's vision port.

The use of two distinctive types of track for the **Tiger,** transportation and combat, had been necessitated by the physical size of the tank itself. Here, the narrower "transportation track" is being fitted prior to this units embarkation by rail for service in another combat zone. The extra road wheels, used with the combat track, will be removed as well.

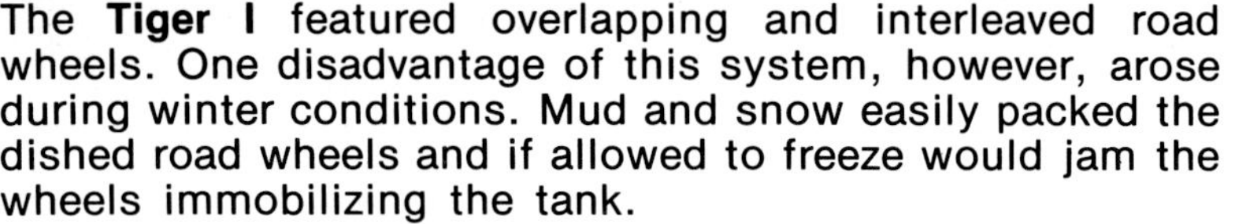

The **Tiger I** featured overlapping and interleaved road wheels. One disadvantage of this system, however, arose during winter conditions. Mud and snow easily packed the dished road wheels and if allowed to freeze would jam the wheels immobilizing the tank.

(Above Right) Placement of the black and white **Balkenkreuz,** national insignia, on the turret is somewhat unusual, even more so with another seen on the rear stowage box! Generally, **Tiger** tanks carried this insignia on the hull sides only. The tank's number "334", red outlined in white, indicates it is the fourth tank of the third platoon of the third company (read number from right to left).

Drive sprockets for the **Tiger** were located forward as was the transmission gear box. The Mayback Olvar preselective transmission provided eight forward and four reverse gear ratios. Shown in this view is not only the drive sprocket, but rear idler along with a dismounted road wheel.

Ammunition used by the **'8.8cm KwK 36'** included High Explosive (**Sprenggranate**) and three types of Armor Piercing (**Panzergranate**) rounds - armor-piercing shell (**Panzergranate**), high explosive armor-piercing shell (**Panzersprenggranate**) and steel armor-piercing shell (**Panzerstahlgranate**). Each type had a specific use and is carefully detailed in a firing table included with the crew's manual.

(Above Left) One of the first pieces of equipment to suffer combat damage on the **Tiger** were the track fenders. Employed only with the wide tracks, these fenders were removable from the sides with the front and rear portions being folded up. The cables stored on the hull sides were used to assist in the mounting of the "battle track", tow cables are located on the top deck.

A fresh supply of ammunition arrives in the standard wicker-type container. Each container holds three rounds and is fitted with a metal plate at either end. Rubber stops protect the shell fuses against jarring. The wicker containers in turn have been shipped in wooden cases for their protection.

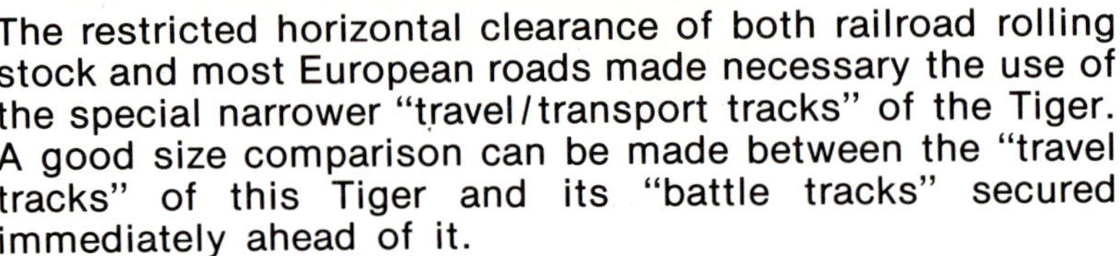

The restricted horizontal clearance of both railroad rolling stock and most European roads made necessary the use of the special narrower "travel/transport tracks" of the Tiger. A good size comparison can be made between the "travel tracks" of this Tiger and its "battle tracks" secured immediately ahead of it.

(Above Right) Interim model **Tiger I** features the improved commander's cupola but retains the earlier model's dished steel disc with solid rubber tired road wheels. Outside road wheels for the wide tracks have been removed for transportation. The wide "battle tracks" were used to decrease the Tiger's ground pressure, an important factor when crossing soft ground.

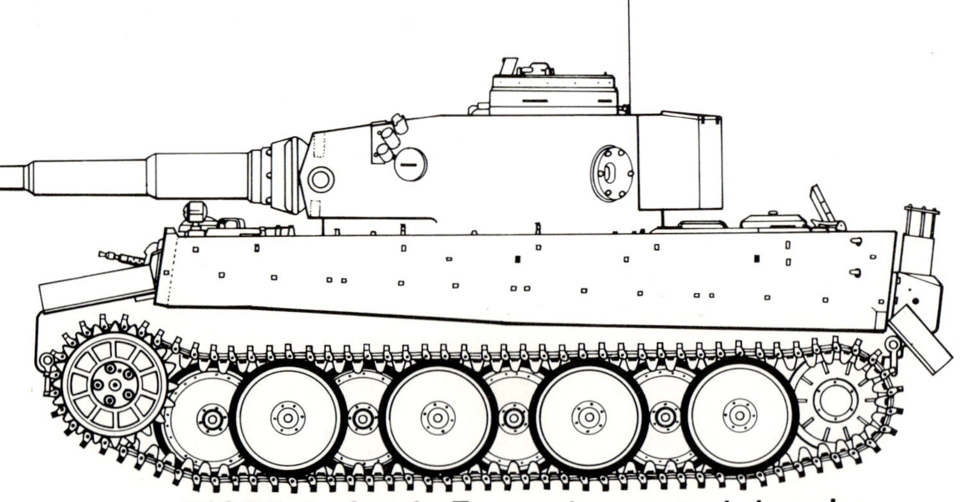

TIGER I Ausf. E on transport tracks.

Stabsfeldwebel (Staff Sergeant-major) examines damage inflicted by a Russian 7.62cm. The 80mm of upper side hull armor has prevented penetration. Armor on the **Tiger** featured interlocking plates welded throughout. Thicknesses were 100mm for the upper and lower hull front and front of turret; 80mm for the hull rear and upper sides, turret rear and side; 60mm lower hull sides and 26mm for all top surfaces and floor.

26mm

60mm

80mm

100mm

Ineffective hit on the driver's plate illustrates one of the recommended defensive maneuvers. When approached by an enemy tank, the driver swung to either the 10:30 or 1:30 clock position, 12:00 facing directly towards the enemy. This movement presented the maximum amount of armor protection of the Tiger to the enemy and also represented the poorest impact angle, roughly 45°.

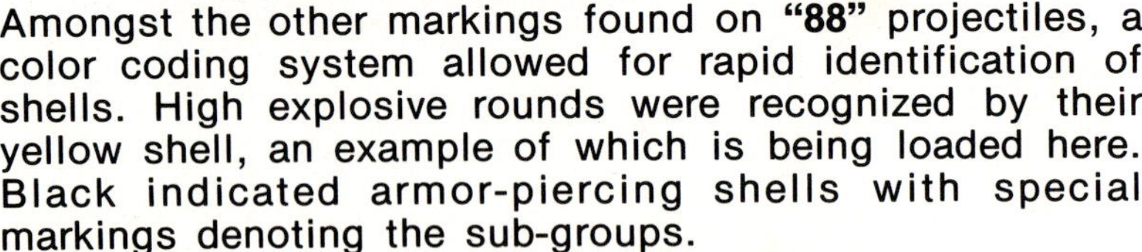

Amongst the other markings found on **"88"** projectiles, a color coding system allowed for rapid identification of shells. High explosive rounds were recognized by their yellow shell, an example of which is being loaded here. Black indicated armor-piercing shells with special markings denoting the sub-groups.

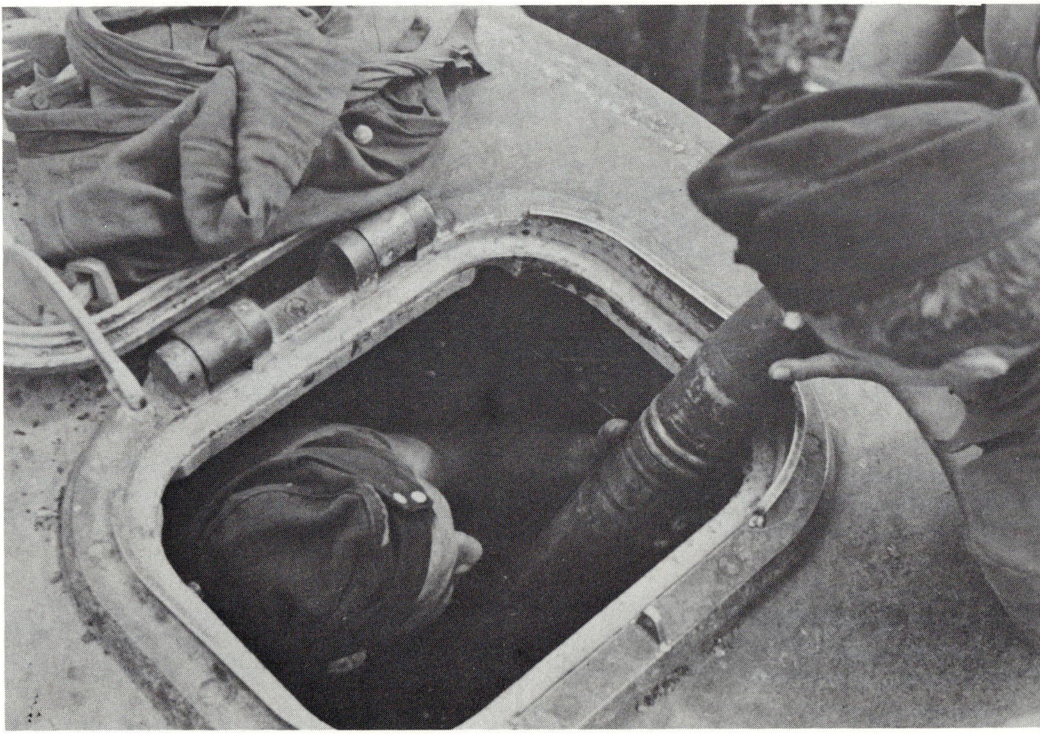

Armor-piercing round, note black projectile marking, is being carefully passed thru the loader's hatch for stowage. While each type of shell had its own specific complete weight, the average **"88"** round remained at about 31 pounds, 20 pounds of which represented the projectile.

Addition of a muzzle brake and electric firing by a trigger on the elevating handwheel marked the prime modifications and differences between the standard 88mm Flak 36 and the 88mm KwK 36 of the **Tiger I.**

Powder residue, and the always present atmospheric dust and dirt, if allowed to collect within the cannon barrel, could cause serious difficulties, i.e. decreased operational life of the weapon's rifling. Replacement of the barrel constituted a major undertaking and required maintenance facilities generally not found available to front line units (see photos on pages 21 and 23).

The care and maintenance of any weapon prolongs its useful life and insures that when called upon for service, will properly function. In this respect there is no difference between an infantryman's rifle and a tanker's vehicle, only that a few more helping hands are needed for cleaning.

"General Winter" was the worst adversary faced by German troops on the Eastern Front. Logistics personnel had been hard pressed to keep up with the needs of the field armies during their rapid expansion into the Russian interior. A steady flow had been maintained during the summer and autumn months. The coming of winter so tremendously increased the difficulties involved in delivery that the safe arrival of every round of ammunition, gallon of fuel, piece of clothing, etc. represented a minor triumph in itself. Note the BMW motorcycle and sidecar in the foreground.

TIGER I in TUNIS

While the 501st Independent Heavy Tank Battalion equipped with **Tiger I's** reached North Africa much too late to alter the outcome of the Allied offensive, the Tigers played an important role in slowing down Allied attacks. Constantly being shifted from one sector to another in order to plug a hole in the German defensive lines, the 88mm weapon of the Tiger I took a terrible toll of Allied armor. Supported by **Panzer III's** and **IV's** the **Tiger I** was first encountered at Pont du Fahs, Tunisia, where both of the attacking Tigers were destroyed by British 6 pounder anti-tank guns. The cumbersome size, mechanical unreliability, and high fuel consumption made them much more potent in the defensive role than one of attack.

Tiger I No. 124 of the Tiger Abteilung 501 was one of the four Tigers entering the battle of Tebourba on December 1, 1942. Two of the Tigers were lost during this battle which ended in favor of the small German Force pushing the 5. British Corps further west while suffering high losses of prisoners and material.

One of the underlying design concepts of German medium tanks, prior to 1936, had been to keep their total weight under that which could be accepted by European bridge load limits. As the weight of tanks grew, so did the problems associated with their transport. Numerous Army Engineer Companies and Russian P.O.W.'s, such as viewed here, assisted in the strengthening of bridges to permit safe passage of the heavies, **Panther, Tiger I and II.**

Panzerkampfwagen VI TIGER I (later version)

Rarely did the **Tigers** operate alone. Adopted policy prescribed the use of two vehicles, mutually supporting the other's flanks. Here, an early model Tiger, lacking the right fender, advances with its companion, an interim model.

Tank "221" ferries a group of **Panzergranadiers** (armored infantry) to the front. Both the Grenadiers and tank crew have been supplied with the two piece reversible winter uniform. This uniform provided not only additional warmth, duly appreciated, but offers two types of camouflage, mouse-gray or white and the standard Army splinter pattern. Tanker standing forward of the parked **Tiger** is wearing the gray side of this jacket out.

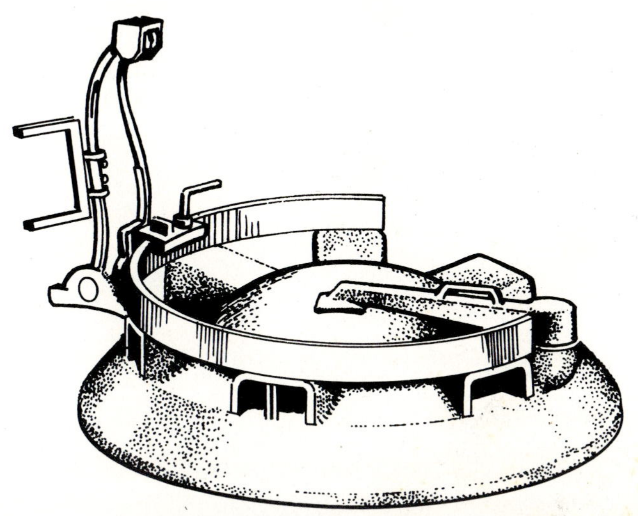

LATE TIGER COMMANDER CUPOLA

The U.S. War Department publication TM-E 30-451 of September 1, 1943 says of the Tiger ". . .a further indication of the general tendency throughout this war towards increased thickness in basic armor, and also armament with increased striking power capable of dealing with hostile tanks". Until the arrival of **Tigers** and **Panthers** in increased numbers, some of the burden of fighting hostile tanks, fell on the shoulders of the **Sturmartillerie.** Never intended to perform against enemy tanks, **Sturmgeschütze**, similar to the one passing a parked interim model Tiger, were with increased frequency called upon to act in an anti-tank role. By the end of 1943 **Sturmgeschütze** had accounted for some 13,000 enemy tanks, a very impressive score!

After a period of running, the heat and exhaust from the **Tiger's** engine would cause the exhaust pipes to glow while emitting a flaming jet of exhaust. A method of rectifying this problem consisted of fitting a deflector plate over the pipes and surrounding them with the circular metal covers as seen here.

Mud conditions produced by autumn rains and snow thawing during the winter, coupled with the primitive Russian road system baulked German mechanized forces. Tracked vehicles could move with minimal difficulty but wheeled vehicles, the most important of which were the supply trucks, bogged down. Panzer effectiveness can be measured by the amount of supplies they received.

PANZERKAMPFWAGEN
ABZEICHEN

The German Ardennes offensive, "Battle of the Bulge", had been a carefully conceived but desperate gamble. Preparations for the offensive had to be conducted under strict secrecy. The stockpiling of large amounts of material, tanks, including Tigers, guns, fuel and the gathering of sufficient troop strength had been accomplished at the expense of Eastern Front forces. A key factor during the ensuing battle was weather. Fog and winter storms allowed the German armored spearheads to operate with immunity from Allied air interdiction.

The **Tigers** first introduction to combat occurred during a minor battle near Leningrad in September 1942. Military leaders the world over held valid the opinion that a new weapon should not be committed to battle until such time as the weapon could be produced in quantity and employed in mass. Hitler, aware of these facts, nevertheless ordered his new weapon, the Tiger, into service. The terrain selected for this operation, swampy forests, prevented any movement other than along the roads. Heavy losses resulted and the fullest advantage of the surprise element, which could have been associated with the Tiger, was forever lost. An inauspicious beginning.

L.A.H.

MICHEL WITTMANN

Wittmann's military career began in October 1934, starting at the bottom of the promotional ladder as a **Schütze,** infantry Private. By 1937 he had entered the **Allgemeine-SS** and been incorporated into their armed branch, known later as the **Waffen-SS.** Assigned to the "LAH", he saw front line duty from September 1939 until his death in 1944 in this division. His first enemy tank kill had been accomplished not with a tank but rather a **Sturmgeschütz,** in which he was also wounded. His kill score and rank steadily progressed. In 1943, Wittmann commanded one of the new Tiger I's and had been commissioned an officer. After his 119th victory and newly promoted to **SS-Obersturmführer,** he was reassigned to duty with **schw. SS-Panzer-Abteilung 101/501** (501st Heavy Tank Battalion), corps troops of the "LAH" Panzer Korps, in the west. His greatest action claim to fame came on June 13, 1944, facing the advancing units of the British 7th Armored Division. His score jumped by 25 destroyed armored vehicles and when later joined by additional German forces, completed the carnage, 138 tanks and 130 AT guns destroyed when the battle ended. The British threat of flanking **Panzer-Lehr Division** was brought to an abrupt halt! His receipt of the Swords to his Knight's Cross on June 22, 1944, can only reflect this impressive feat. Continuing to fight in the invasion area, Wittmann was reported missing in action on August 8, 1944. Indications, concerning his death, are that he and his crew were caught in one of the massed carpet bombing raids used to assist Allied ground forces make their breakout from the bridgehead area.

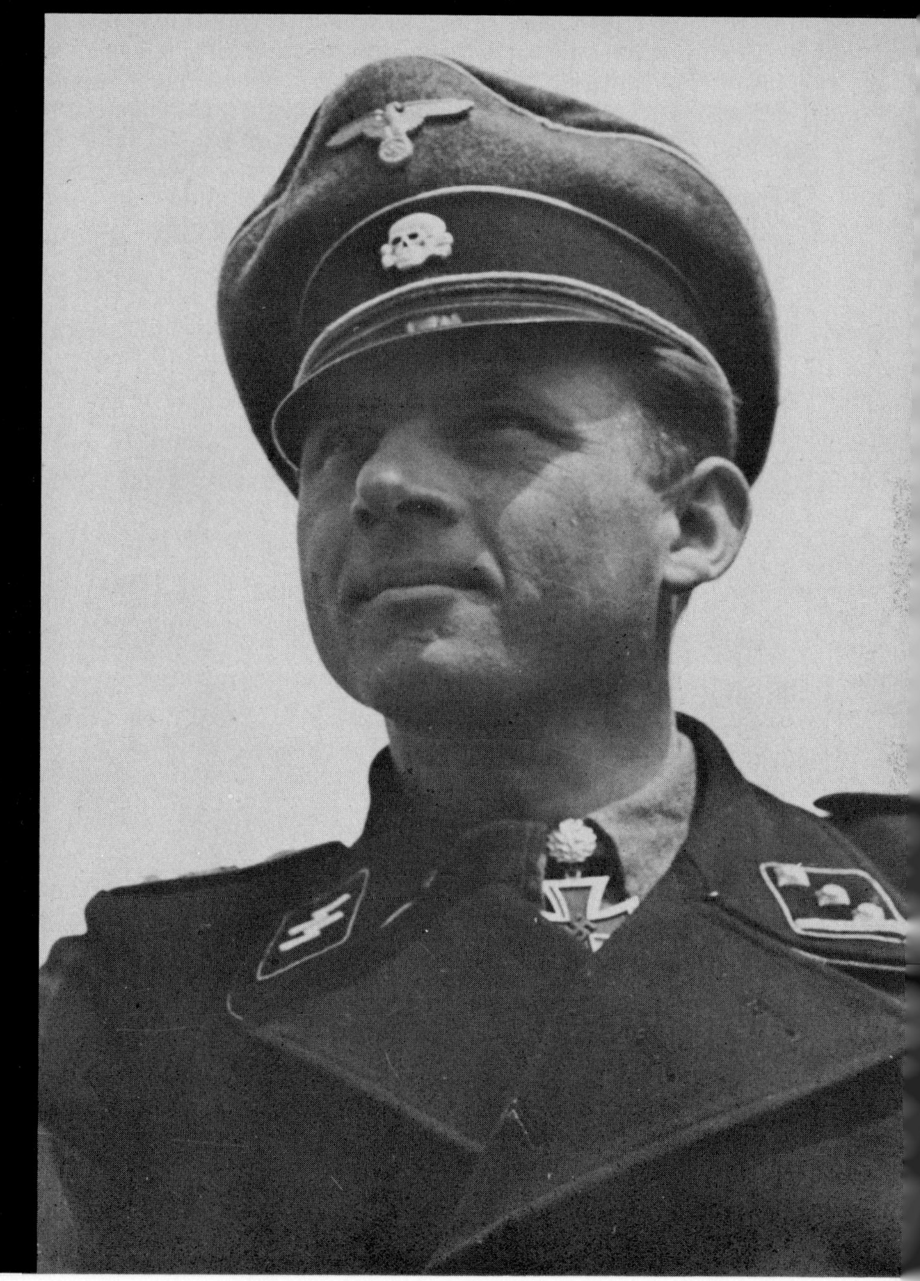

Wittmann receives a light from his gunner, **SS-Oberscharführer** Balthasar Woll. It is believed that this particular photo was taken on the occassion of Wittmann's receipt of the Oak Leaves to the Knight's Cross, January 30, 1944. The Oak Leaves had been presented in recognition of eighty-eight confirmed tank kills and followed only 17 days after he had received the Ritterkreuz for the destruction of his first sixty-six vehicles, the latter award having been considerably delayed. At the time of these awards, Wittmann and his crew were members of the **I. SS-Panzer-Korps "Leibstandarte SS Adolf Hitler".** The distinctive embroidered slip-on "LAH" monogram shoulder strap denoted the **I.SS-Panzer Division "Leibstandarte SS Adolf Hitler",** not to be confused with the Korps. Officers' monogram appeared in metal. "LAH" division members were the only Waffen-SS formation to wear special insignia on their shoulder straps.

Adolf Hitler

As the war dragged on, the suitability of the all black panzer uniform grew less and less. Black made an exceptional target and readily pointed up panzer units as being in the vicinity. Both Army and Waffen-SS armored formation were issued with camouflaged versions of their previous uniform, using their respective standard camouflage patterns. Here, Wittmann's driver wears such a uniform, one of four autumn patterns but in summer colors, along with the Iron Cross First Class, Tank Assault Badge and shoulder straps indicating "LAH" division.

Wittmann's gun crew, loader and gunner, Balthasar Woll. Much of Wittmann's success resulted from the cooperation and combined effort on the part of his crew. Like Wittmann, Woll has also been awarded the Knight's Cross, a rare distinction for enlisted or NCO ranks, and the Iron Cross First Class, barely visible over the hatch cover.

Tigers of the **'schw. SS-Pz.-Abt. 101/501'**, corps troops of the **I. SS-Panzer-Korps 'Leibstandarte SS Adolf Hitler'.** The recovery of a comrade-in-arms often resulted in the tanks themselves towing damaged vehicles, an act strictly against regulations.

(Far Right) On the morning of June 6, 1944 only ten panzer and panzergrenadier divisions were stationed within the whole of France. Four of these divisions operated under General Rommel's command with an additional three in OKW reserve. The Allied landings in Normandie took place within Rommel's command area and though he personally was absent at the time, his forces began counterattacks and the panzer divisions were ordered to mass for the maximum effort. Permission from the OKW to move the three reserve armored divisions to an attack position was not forthcoming. It was felt that this Allied assault represented a bluff on their part, the "real" invasion would come in the Pas de Calais sector.

Cavalry throughout its history had been used for its shock effect and by virtue of its mobility, reconnaissance, sudden charges and long raids. These identical duties were undertaken by the modern armored unit. For the most part, tanks had replaced the horse mounted soldier. An exception to this is found on the Eastern Front. The Russians fielded large cavalry formations. German cavalry units were not as large but efforts were made to expand these forces. Many times, only tanks and horses could traverse the vastness which is Russia.

205

The Corps insignia of **I. SS-Panzer-Korps** is clearly illustrated on the driver's plate, viewed to the right of the driver's vision port. The vehicle has been completely coated with anti-magnetic plaster, **"Zimmerit",** with the exception of the area in which the insignia appears.

By mid-1944, the German Luftwaffe had lost its control over western European air space. The R.A.F. and U.S.A.A.F. were the rulers of the skies, coming and going at will. This change of events is reflected even in the panzer divisions. The installation of AA machine-gun mounts on the commander's cupola, seen here, had been required so that the panzers could themselves offer some measure of self-defense against attacks from the **'Jabos',** Allied fighter-bombers.

LEIBSTANDARTE SS
ADOLF HITLER

Corps troops included communications battalion, military police, security company and field post office. Apart from these service and security units, specific combat units were attached directly to the Corps proper along with additional specialized service groups. Numerical designations of these units were derived by adding their parent corps' number to a base of 100. As such, **'schw. SS-Pz.-Abt. 101/501'** meant Heavy Tank Battalion 501, corps troops of the **I. SS-Panzer-Korps.**

The paper strength establishment of a Heavy Tank Battalion included 27 officers, 216 NCO's, 406 enlistedmen, 3 quad 20mm self-propelled AA flak tanks, 45 Tigers, 127 motor vehicles, 8 of these armored, and 18 motorcycles. Tank strength in the three Tank Companies of this Battalion varied between 14 and 17 per Company.

By the end of 1943, the established tank strength per armored division had again been reduced from previous levels. Although German industry had finally been geared to the war effort, principally through the effort of Albert Speer, Minister for Armaments, it was hard pressed to meet the demands of the Eastern Front and the beginnings of the Allied march in Europe. Hitler continually demanded the creation of new armor divisions, ever increasing the production burden. Several exceptions to this general reduction in force existed. Elite Army and Luftwaffe units, such as **Panzer-Lehr** and **Herman Goering Divisions** and the greater majority of Waffen-SS units, who could exert pressure through political maneuverings, generally fielded far stronger armor elements than found in other "normal" areas. The Volkswagen **'Schwimmwagen',** foreground, performed yeoman duty within the armored divisions.

Panzerkampfwagen VI TIGER I

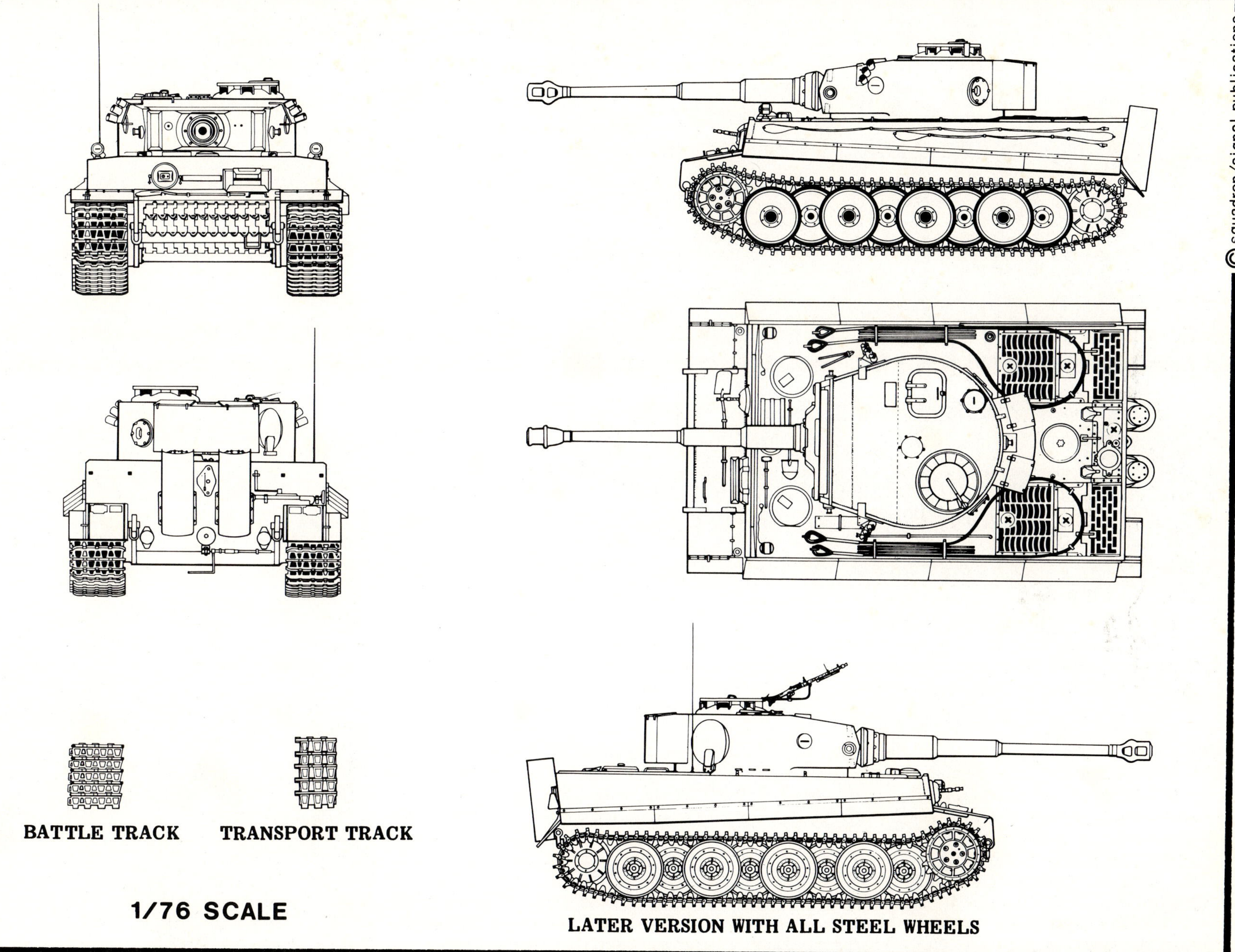

LATER VERSION WITH ALL STEEL WHEELS

SQUADRON
SIGNAL
PUBLICATIONS
SIGNAL Panzer III IN ACTION
Luftwaffe Bombers
in Action
F4 Phantom II
in Action
Fallschirmjäger
in
ACTION
SOVIET PANZERS
in Action
PANZERJÄGER in Action
Luftwaffe in Action
Part 4
squadron/signal publications
AIRCRAFT NO. EIGHT $3.95